Cracked but not Broken....

Leslie Humphrey

Presentation by *BookLeaf Publishing*

Web: www.bookleafpub.com

E-mail: info@bookleafpub.com

ISBN: 9789357212434

First edition 2023

DEDICATION

I dedicate this book to my best friend (may she rest in peace) Tami Inman. She pushed me to move forward with this. When i doubted myself she was there with encouragment.. She had faith in my success even when i did not .. I wish she was here with me now to see that i did it ... So i dedicate this book to her.   I love you and you will be missed!! Rip# Tami Inman

ACKNOWLEDGEMENT

This is a life long dream of mine. Ive always believed there was a reason why i was put through all i was put through through out my life and i believe that this book will open the doors needed for me to achieve all my goals.

Whats it mean?

I am cracked but not broken, but what does that
really mean? Could it be the venom that spewed
from her lips that left me many nights asking
"why are you treating me like this ?
Or could it be that the teasing i endured
.growing up had left an invisable scar across my
heart and gave me my inability to trust? I am
cracked but not broken so who are you to judge
? Because as i recall all those nights in that hall
when my grandpa would lay down and say "
This is what kids do , its not a big deal keep
quiet as grandpa plays. Cracked but not broken
so sad but its true , how every boyfriend i ever
had promised to be the new , on the outside
looking in he seemed devoted and true but
behind closed doors the monsters raged grew ..
Cracked but not broken the scars that i have tell
the story of a war. The physical and emotional
abuse that was inflicted on me made me believe
this life was more of a fantasy than reality....

Unwanted

Thats what i felt from my earliest memory of my life growing up in hell.. Kind words and soft touches were not part of my normal day.. Instead it was more me hiding in my closet wishing the monsters away....
When we think of monsters we think of those we seen on tv , But my real life monster was much worse then that for my monster was always suppose to have my back...My monster had a name and a face i knew all too well.. My monster showed me no mercy while i was put through hell.. Leaving me broken , nothing more than a empty shell..
Unwanted is the word i felt the most, unsure of myself , feeling unsafe. . My monster was my caregiver how do you come back from that?
Could not understand at my very young age how the people who claim to love me could ever treat me this way... As the days turn into months and months into years, follow my story and ill lay out all my fears ..Just follow me around here and my story line will start to appear...... I was unwanted from the start and nothing ever changed . . ill still be unwanted even from my grave...

My Fear

My fear at times can be so overwhelming..
Trapping me within my mind, my legs wont
move , at times im frozen to where i stand.. Im
looking for a safe place to land.
The monsters in my life has left me completely
alone.. Scared to death to let someone in scared
to try to make a home...My fear has me
convinced there is no better for me than this.
The fairy tale type of love i longed for , The
happily ever after bliss. I have always wanted to
feel... It can get so bad that i see things in a
different way then most. Everyone is out to hurt
me, No one to make me whole....
My fear has cost me everything . my freedom,
my kids, my love.. My fear is always with me ,
we go hand in hand (fits like a glove) My fear
stems back many years ago and through the
years has only grown .. How do i let it go, turn
an
 walk away.. Fear can be crippling. Scared to go,
scared to stay. No one would understand this ..
Tell me how could they? To know where my
fear came from and how deeply rooted ..
Nobody to share this with , to ashamed to admit

its true and that my fear sometimes controls me
and makes me do things i never wanted to do.

Cried out

I cried out to no one .....
But everyday i cried ....
I cried out to no one ....
Cause everybody lies....
I cried out to no one....
Who would be there anyway...
I cried out to no one...
No one to take this pain away....
I cried out to no one .
All those lonely nights alone ....
I cried out to no one.....
No place to call a home....
I cried out to no one. .
Though i wanted someone to see me and all this
pain i held inside.....
I cried out to no one. .
Cause i had no one to cry out too...
I cried out to no one ...
Not even you......

The simple things

Its the simple things i long for... The things most do not even think twice about ..
The simple things i have done without for many many years .. A smile, A kind word, A soft gentle embrace...
A simple hello could all make my bad day turn and go a different way....
The simple things , A kiss, a touch, a safe play to lay. I long for simple pleasures.. Ones that come so easily to others.. The ones i was denied all my life from one person to another ..
The simple pleasures , getting a house , a car etc... Knowing what it feels like to be needed to be cared for. The simple day to day things that make life a little sweeter. The simple things in life the things most will ignore .is the things i crave the most .. The things that i adore ...

See Me

See me .. The real me .. The me i dont let others see..
See me beyond my flaws and my scars ...
See me for the broken woman i am , Who has come to far.. See me and see i have been hurt behind the hands of men.
See me and see my insecurity, see my doubts, see my fears, and embrace me for the next 10 to 15 years.
See me and fall in love with every stretch mark with every wrinkle with every strand of new grey hair.   See me and show me how to love you properly .show me what it feels like to be loved. See me and see my soul see my heart on my sleeve .see me and see the many people who have taken advantage of me.   See me and want to give be better... See me behind the pain in my eyes and understand why its so hard to let go. .
See me and see your forever .. Together we can grow...

Forgive me

Forgive me for my mistakes both big ones and the small too... Forgive me for making bad choices when i knew not what to do....
Forgive me for not knowing better and making better decisions.. Forgive me for my mental illnesses anxiety and depression.... Forgive me for hating myself and not like what i see when i look in the mirror. .
Forgive me that i hate myself for all that i have been through .. Forgive me for not being paranoid and isolating myself from the world. Forgive me for being a woman but inside a trapped little girl..
Forgive me for not knowing how to say i am sorry or regulating any kind of emotion.. The people in my life before this moment has always been mean .. Forgive me if i seem a little distant .. Im just watching the whole scence fold out before me ..
Forgive me for thinking that everyone is out to get me . But when you have been through the horror i have been through you start to realize and believe certain things. Forgive me for constantly asking for forgiveness.. Its a coping mechanism.. Forgive me for this and for

anything more . forgive me for forgiving you
and brushing u back out the door...

Numb

At times i get so numb i can no longer feel a
thing .
My hands no longer tinkle, my knee's no longer
weak. My heart does not race. . No thoughts at
all Eveything is blank.. I have been completely
numb that i could no longer smile . I no longer
felt the need to even get out of bed and shower.
When you go numb with no feelings thats when
life becomes the scariest. I did not know if i was
sad or mad or up or down.
Ive been numb for so long i dont know how to
let myself feel. I have been so numb for so long
i do not know how to let myself feel. I have
been so numb that i couldnt even shed a tear . I
had to become numb to survive from day to day.
My feelings overwhelmed me . My past
trauma"s caused me some pain.. After years of
fight or flight mode 24/7 i had become so numb
i could no longer be myself..
And with each new relationship the same pattern
started to emerge maybe eveey one else was
right and i was not worthy of some love.. I had
to close off my heart and put ice in our veins.
.Nobody would understand. So why even try to
explain.....

Take me as i am

Take me as i am , with all my broken pieces, I am flawed and i have scars from the hell from which i was seated.
Take me as i am , i will find it hard to believe that you love me ...and ill always need reasurance . You will have to be really patient and at times you wont think its worth it.
Take me as i am , Be gentle and be kind. Ive known the feelings of rage and ive felt a hand thats not been kind ..
Take me as i am., Show me there is still good in this world , Show me how i should be treated, give me somethimg more to believe in .. .
Take me as i am, Teach me how to love , take me in your arms and promise you will cause no harm.. Be that person i can count on who will never let me down.. Keep a smile on my face so that i never have to frown.
Take me as i am , Show me how to best love you i am learning as i go.. This is all new to me so lets just take it slow. And please dont let me go....

I hate you

I hate you.. Them words seem so hard to hear but i assure you I hate you i can say without sheding a tear ..
I hate you for all the lies and the pain you put me through.
I hate you for sure and there"s no more you and me.
I hate you for all the times you made me cry .
All the tines you had me feelimg so bad that all i wanted to do was die
I hate you for all the times you ever put me down or made me feel worthless. And i hate you so much for telling me it would all be worth it ...I hate you for all the times you cheated on me , then look me in my face said if i didnt like it i could leave... I hate you for holding me back , had me scared of my own potential , Damn your love was so determental... I hate you for all the times you made me believe that you were mine forever and that youd never leave .
But most of all I hate me for not seeing you for the monster that you are . I hate you for allowing me to turn back into the frightened little girl i once was.. I hate you for everytime you made me bleed , every slap, every punch ,every hair

pull, and every neck squeeze .. I hate you for all
of this and so much more..And i will hate you
for life.. Rest assured i dont want no more... Just
know that i hate you and ill hate you till i die ...
Couldnt stop with the cheating , couldnt stop
with the lies ......

Alone

Even when i am in a room full of people i am still alone.. A completely empty feeling is how to best say it. So alone even though theres always some body around . They all have bad intentions and only let me down.
So alone .. I felt this way for most of my life. A lot of bad things have happened so if i get a all clear i wont think twice. We could maybe start over doing it right this time. Maybe i can help change our days... And our nights .. I am so alone i have no one to hold. No place to call home. Stay with me tonight and tomarrow too. Never let me go and ill never be blue.. I am so alone scared of my own mind . Dont know which way to turn , feels like i am losing my mind ! Come be my peace, and silence my nagging mind.   Come to my place so i wont be alone tonight.

I am sorry

I am sorry you found it so hard to love me even in my early days .. Sorry that you rather go have more kids while you gave me away.. Im sorry that when you look at me you cant stand what you see. I remind you of my daddy thats why you feel this way toward me ..
Im sorry i gave you such a hard time . Even though i was only asking for you not to treat me that way .. I asked only for love ..Some how this was my fault everything always gets blamed on me . Thats why i am constantly saying i am sorry to everyone i meet..
I have been conditioned to believe that everything bad that has happened in my life has always been my fault. So i walked on egg shells each and everyday .. Scared to death i might fall..
I am sorry . Two words i have said millons of times. . I felt so bad about myself that i was saying im sorry for just even existing.. Saying im sorry for being so worthless. . So im telling you   im sorry ahead of time , In hopes that you will stay. When you realize how screwd up i am ill be saying sorry anyway.

It was not my fault

Some words strung together and get spoken
many times a day. It wasnt my fault is what
every teenager would say.. .
But to someone who has been abused in any way
them words take on a whole new meaning.
It was not my fault nobody loved me growing up
and it was not my fault grandpa liked little girls
or that he couldnt help himself from touching
me.   It was not my fault my brother decided to
take his own life or that day he died i almost
died too.. It was not my fault after that when i no
longer cared about anything.. .not even
school.But I was ok. Kept saying i am sorry as
his hand connected with my face. It was not my
fault that i felt so alone cause the lonelyness is
all i know.
Its not my fault i feel like this cause i was never
shown no different .

Friends

Friends are hard to come by in these times were
living in. Real friends like we used to have
many many years ago. When i was growing up
the friends were much different . They were real
and loyal and would fight in your honor toe to
toe. Friends back then called your momma
mom.. And when we played we played jump
rope and hop scotch.. We had to come in the
house when the street lights came on .. But these
friends these days only care of themselves .. Not
there mom not there kids not anyone else.
The world today is different and people in the
world too.. So be cautious when you let
someone in , most friends arent here to
stay.....they come with false intentions not to
brighten up your day. Keep these friends at arm
length until you truely get to see id these friends
are really friends and not pretending to be

My demons

My demons are powerful.. A force like no other... My demons get in deep.. Deeper than anyome else. They pretended to be my friend . There is one waiting around every bend.
I cant run and i cant hide ... For my demons they came to fight . My demons always tell me how i cant do nothing right.. And i may as well give up this fight .
My demons know my fears, my regrets my mistakes... He knows how much my body can take. These demons are like my shadow always there close .. Sometimes they give me comfort when i need it the most. They are always with me no matter where i go. My demons are always around ...

He said

He said that he loved me and he would always be here... He said we have forever so let go of all of your fears ..
He said lets make a family , start a life and be alone..So excited for this new beginning that i ignored what i had seen all along . He said be my wife and we can share everything . Little did i know this man was going to turn out so mean.. I walked on egg shells and seldom did i smile . . I forgot who i was and my life no longer worth wild . He said he loved me but he lied.. Cause he could never love me and live in denial. This man was a monster who simply did not care .. He punch , he scratch and even pulled my hair.. I waited for a savior but none came my way . i was trapped and i was tortured i never wanted my life to be this way .. How do i break free . how do i let go.. This man no longer is the person that i know .. He said he loved me but he did lie ... Cant take no more of this its time to say goodbye ....

Lessons

Life has so many lessons . Some are hidden
others are not . Some lessons are meant to teach
other lessons are meant to be blessings..But no
matter which it is there is always something to
be learned..
Our lessons begin at a very early age . And keep
on coming to our dying day. What we take from
them is up to us .. We can get down low or have
a stroke of luck .
I take my lessons and i hold them deep. Cause i
know these lessons were just made for me .
Although some i may understand I have to
accept them cause thats just the way i am . Life
can get hard but its worth the struggle so take
your lessons along with the blessings .. Learn
from your mistakes and make a change .. Your in
control and your lessons arent to blame ...

The comeback

My comeback will be hard. Things will not be so easy .. But my comeback will show my progress on how much i have grown. My comeback will be epic and i dont expect everyone to understand... But my comeback is for all my haters who said i would never make it anyway .. For all the people who said i should go another way .. My comeback will make people mad but i dont care either way.. No body was there to catch me when i fell.
My comeback will be worth the scars i got in my hell . My comeback is my victory and this i will not fail...

Losing my best friend

Losing my best friend wasnt planned and came unexpected. And it is unbearable pain. She was a angel walking amongst monsters and we as people burnt out her light. She was to good for this world. My best friend taught me the meaning of patience and understanding. Showed me how to love everyone and not to pass judgement . Her beautiful soul held no hate or greed cuz love is all she has known. If you were blessed to have met her she would make you feel at home . Thats one of the reasons i hate that she is gone..Cause her home is the only home i have known...

Trust again

Before i can trust again i must first learn to work
on myself for i must trust myself before i learn
to trust someone else.
My trust has been broken a thousand times
over.... I trust no one . not a single living soul.
To trust again it will take patience, and reading
all the signs. To trust again i must surrender to
loving someone else again...
To trust again will take honesty , respect , and
communication. Alot of bridges were burnt with
trust so i am a little ruff around the edges ..
To trust again i must first see something i can
hold onto cause i cant take you at your word.
To trust again will take time . it is not something
we can rush .To trust again we must follow
intition and listen to our gut .. You must learn
how or the lonelyness will become to much to
bear .. It will be a long bumpy ride back to
where i trust again but i am willing to put in
effort if your willing to put in a helping hand .

The new beginning

24

Worked through some issues, know what i need to do.. Its time for a fresh start , a new beginning , some where to start anew..
I survied the harshs places and suffered the most punishment and abuse to get to where i am today.   Took alot of work and hardly no play, i overcame things that were meant to take me down.
But i came at it face to face never not once breaking down. And i faught with all i had , no way could i ever run now. I overcame it and got better. The sun was shining again. I learned how to slow down to finally breath. This new beginning has so much meaning
A new start , a brighter day. This new beginning gave me something to believe in and for once i looked forward to another day... My fight is far from over but i will fight to the end . om hopes of encouraging others to do the same.